THE TRUE ACCOUNT OF HOW LIFE CAME ABOUT

THE BIBLICAL CREATION STORY

EXPANDED WITH

THE WISDOM OF EDGAR CAYCE'S READINGS

AND

TRANSLATIONS OF THE SUMERIAN TABLETS

Read-aloud Rhymes

by Lenore Vinyard Bechtel

Illustrations and Cover

by Mallory Noelle

Copyright 2021 by Lenore Vinyard Bechtel

All rights reserved. No part of this book may be reproduced, stored in a retrieval system, or transmitted in any form or by any means without the prior written permission of the publisher, except by a reviewer who may quote brief passages in a review to be printed in a newspaper, magazine , or journal.

First printing

ISBN: 9781735703954

Library of Congress Control Number: 2020917058

Published by

Write-On Creations
15235 Scenic Woodland Drive
Conroe, TX 77384

For the Reader

Edgar Cayce, the most documented psychic of the 20th century, was unquestionably in touch with an infinite intelligence that channeled truths to him to help mankind. Some of that wisdom expands upon the Bible's creation stories in the first two chapters of Genesis.

Zecharia Sitchin translated the Sumerian Tablets, which revealed creation stories written more than 20,000 years ago— many centuries before the Bible. The Sumerian stories have many similarities but also variances to the Biblical version of how life started on earth.

Information from Cayce and Sitchin contribute to this read-aloud story, which is followed by an addendum of quotations that support this creation narrative.

Tell me, tell me-- who are we?
Why are you all I can see?

I am Father, you are Son,
Two together, but still one.

Tell me, father, tell me how
I'm myself but look like thou?

I dreamed you to be like me,
In my image, don't you see?

Did you dream me all alone?
Am I all you've ever known?

Yes, you are, and you I love,
We'll have fun up here above.

Tell me, tell me--where are we?
Is this where we'll always be?

It's the place I first put here,
Don't you like the atmosphere?

I like it fine but I'd like more,
More souls like us I would adore.

Thoughts are things that manifest,
We can think what we want best.

All I want is just to see
More than only you and me.

Your wish, my son, I will fulfill,
Look down, look up-- for a big thrill

Those morning stars that shine so bright
Have me inside them in their flight,
Their souls are just like yours and mine
They have free will by my design.

Tell me, tell me—what's free will?
Does it take a lot of skill?

No, it means they
get to choose.
Whether they will
win or lose.

Win at what—the
games we play?
I'll let them win so
they will stay.

Soon enough you'll
come to know
Why you might have to
let them go.

Those star souls came for us to love,
Companions for us up above,
My word is law. I'm everything,
Would you like those stars to sing?

To hear music in my ears
Would fill me up with boundless cheers.

Then I'll think big and thus disperse
Some thoughts to make a universe.

Oh my, oh my—what's that I feel?
My heart has told me something real.

"Let there be light,"
that's what I thought.
Enlightenment
is what you got.

Did all these star souls get the same?
Do they now know from whence they came?

They do! Let's hope they'll want to stay
And play with you each joyful day.

But look, but look—some go away,
Why would they want to go astray?

They don't recall why
they were born,
Their selfishness makes
me forlorn.

But you yourself gave them free will,
They use it now, our fun to kill.

Look where they've
gone—the very place
The sun does shine
from my good grace.

Hear how loudly each soul sings?
Did you project those pretty things?

You, my son, could create same,
Thought project what e'er you name.
I thought that ocean's water clear
And trees to make that planet dear.
Some life that lives only down there,
A fish, a dog, a cow, a bear.

I'll thought project a scaly hide
With tail so long and mouth so wide
It could gulp down those pretty trees
And dominate all that it sees.

Be careful, son, what you ask for,
That dinosaur you might abhor.
These animals are like our souls,
They have free will to chase their goals.

Their world down there
will be their own,
Their loss to us
I do bemoan.

No no, my son, don't feel that way,
The Law of One they've cast away,
And if they do not want to stay,
We mustn't force them to obey.

They must remember who they are,
To come back to us from afar.

Oh look, a giant stands so straight,
A mermaid swims to find her bait.

They've thought projected into things
To make themselves like earthly beings.

But they are gross!
That unicorn
is making my soul
feel forlorn.

To switch to matter in such ways,
makes bodies bad for earthly days.
Let's hope they change the way they choose,
If not, the fun they seek, they'll lose.

So many years have passed down there
So many souls their skills did share
And they've built countries, one called Mu
Plus fine Atlantis thriving too.

Alas, their bodies are so gross
Seeing them makes me morose,
Send me, dear father, for their sake,
To see them makes my sad heart break.
Let me project a better shell
For them to wear while in this spell.

Remind them that we dwell in bliss,
Remind them of the fun they miss.
But if they want to stay on earth,
They must have bodies with more worth.

Oh please, dear father, make a plan
For them to come back when they can.

To do so they will have to learn
Some lessons in their earth's sojourn.

The lesson is to you they owe
All that they have and all they know.

Their earthly lives they must repeat
Until they give up all conceit.
Now you may go, though I'll miss you.
Thought project as you can do,
Create a body we'll call man,
Phase out the monsters as you can.
Teach them to live with righteousness
And then I once again will bless.

I'll call myself Amilius,
Life's truths with them I will discuss.
I'll guide them toward the light of life,
And help them with their wordly strife.

My son then to Atlantis went
And many earthly years he spent,
While still in spirit he found out
What earthly souls thought most about.

For they forgot their home up here
And held material most dear.
Amelius himself fell prey
To yearnings in an earthly way.

His mission, though, he did pursue
Getting much earned ballyhoo.
Most earthly spirits he set free
From their entanglement ennui.

He saw how beasts could birth their own
And felt each soul should so be shown.
He thought projected a female.
Lilith he loved for he was male.

All souls did same and each learned how
To make his very own sweet frau.
Then babies came into the clan.
I call them Sons and Daughters of Man.

Oh, Father dear, I feel I failed,
My plans to get them back derailed.

I'm sorry while they stay down there
They're missing pleasures everywhere
Because their bodies physically
Are not as good as they could be.

They cannot smell or taste or feel,
Delights of senses are not real.
I wish I'd thought a better form
Than what has now become the norm.

Dear son, I hate to tell you this,
While you were gone, more fell from bliss.
I need to send some souls from God,
To thrive where awful thought forms trod.

Each soul up here has triple parts,
The mind goes where the shape departs.
But they don't get their souls unless
I alone agree to bless.

The sons of God revere their souls,
Belials, though, have other goals.
They defy the Law of One,
Their evil now must be undone.

I will not give them souls until
They all agree to do my will.
I'll send star souls who choose to go,
To five locations down below.

Oh holy God, trust me to go
To help those prisoners below.
I'll go as Adam, earth's first man,
Conceived in spirit with a plan
To think good bodies for their use
To show them how to reproduce.
To help them spend their sojourns well
Until they come back here to dwell.

Go, my son, but spread the word.
Let the rules of law be heard,
Whate'er they give will bounce right back,
If they do good, they'll never lack.
But if they're selfish, full of greed,
They'll never have all that they need.

I'd like to add another law,
That each must hold you in their awe.
Each must adore and love thyself,
And love his neighbor as himself.

To Atlantis I will go
To join those lost from God below,
To be the first made from earth's dust,
To free them from lives so unjust.

And so it was that Adam led
A swarm of souls who chose to spread
   Where they were needed down below
   In the five spots where they would go,

        The climate of the place they went
        Made skin to be a special tint.
           T'is Yellow in a waterless place,
           The Gobi desert for their race.

Carpathia will Eden be
Home for white fertility.
   Blacks can thrive in climates hot
   So Africa did get their lot.

        Andean mountains are the home
        Down south for browns who need no dome.
           Light red are the Atlanteans
           And also the Americans.

Each color signifies a drive
With which each entity will thrive.
Whites will have their vision clear,
The yellow race the most will hear.

Blacks with tastebuds that excel
Browns with noses sharp with smell.
Reds with feelings, strong with touch,
To each race I've given much.

Eons had passed before they went
And found that others had been sent,
In steamy Africa they found
The gold they needed did abound.

The planet Nibiru had air
The Anunnaki did despair,
But gold could purify it well
And make their planet fit to dwell.

They felt themselves much too high-souled
To work themselves to mine for gold,
So they combined their DNA
With earthly beasts who had no say.

And thus the blacks that God had sent
Found slaves who suffered discontent.
While Adam in Atlantis found
Souls entangled all around.

Thus Adam went but was too late
To save Atlantis from its fate.
Belial bums with hate prevailed
And worldly progress was derailed,

They harnessed sunrays to a stone
That caused their island to be blown.
Atlantis met catastrophe,
Became five isles and then just three,
The great flood sunk the very last one
But most Atlaneans were gone.

Adam to Carpathia fled,
And yearned for a fair maid to wed.
So he pulled Eve out from his side,
In Eden then they did reside.

Their garden held all they might seek,
This pair was truly quite unique,
The last man that had *not* been made
With the first helpmeet that *was* made.

Eve gave birth to baby Cain,
Then Abel came to their domain,
Son Seth then joined the family tree
Which now includes both you and me.

Relationships could now begin
With all the sons and daughters of men.

Remember yellow, brown, and black
Received the knowledge they had lacked

And so in spots where souls had gone
All Sons of God made two from one.

Now all could do as animals showed
And welcome babies to their fold.

Those bad guys who were called Belial,
From their own sins were in denial.
Untouchables they then became
And others treated them as shame.

For years they never changed their ways,
Untouchables received no praise.
They had to serve the better guys
Until they learned to be as wise.

This tale of birth you need not doubt
For this is how life came about.
Each person born has me inside
For help, before they then reside
As my companion where I live
With many blessings here to give.

For in our hearts we all are one,
And all are mine to fawn upon.
All that I ask is don't misdo,
Love me as much as I love you,
Love others too, and if you do
You'll have fun and blessings too.

EDGAR CAYCE QUOTATIONS FROM HIS READINGS

PAGE 1:

He is to be the Master, the Christ, sufficient unto every soul, the MAKER the CREATOR of all that is in this sphere! The LORD of all! 254-71

No matter in what clime, under what name, all must come to that as was from the beginning. For, know that He - who was lifted up on the Cross in Calvary - was also that Son in the land of the setting sun; also he that first walked among men at the beginning of man's advent into flesh! For He indeed was and is the first Adam, the last Adam; that is the way, the truth, the light! 2402-2

PAGE 4:

In the beginning was the word. The words was God. He MOVED! 263-13

PAGE 5:

Hence as He moved, Souls—portions of Himself—came into being. 263-19

PAGE 6:

….in the beginning was the word, the Word WAS with God, the Word WAS God, the same was IN the beginning. 364-7

PAGE 7:

Then a soul—the offspring of the Creator—entering into a consciousness which becomes a manifestation in any plane or sphere of activity, is given free will for its use of those abilities or qualities or conditions in its experience. 5753-1

So, before Creation there was Spirit. The Spirit comes down…into the Physical Body; and returns, starting from the Cells, to build through the Physical to the Spirit again. With this picture we see exactly what was meant … it said Spirit was the beginning and the end of all steps for a soul's development, in the earth. Also we understand the Spirit of Jesus Christ saying in the vision to John, "I am Alpha and Omega, the Beginning and the End, the first and the last." 281-63

PAGE 9.

The First Cause was that the created would be the companion for the Creator, that is the creature, show itself to be not only worthy of, but companionable to, the Creator. 5753-1

PAGES 10 & 11:

...in the beginning, when all forces were given in the spiritual force, and the morning stars sang together in the glory of the coming of the Lord and the God to make the giving of man's influence and developing in the world's forces. 2497-1

When the forces of the universe came together, upon the waters was the sound of the coming of the songs of God. And the morning stars sang together. Over the face of the waters was the voice of the glory of the coming of the plane for man's indwelling. The earth in its form became a place; and afterwards able to be an abode for the creature called man. 341-1

First that of a mass, which there arose the mist, and then the rising of same with light breaking OVER that as it SETTLED itself, as a companion of those in the universe, as it began its NATURAL (or now natural) rotations, with the varied effects UPON the various portions of same, as it slowly - and is slowly - receding or gathering closer to the sun, from which it receives its impetus for the awakening of the elements that give life itself, by radiation of like elements from that which it receives from the sun. 364-6

PAGE 13:

The highest SPIRITUAL Attribute is Light. The first creation was Light. If our Soul continues to follow the light, we will get back to our Source. 281-63

He, that Christ-Consciousness, is that first spoken of in the beginning when God said, "Let there be light, and there was light." And that is the light manifested in the Christ. First it became physically conscious in Adam. 2879-1

...God moved and said, "Let there be light," and there was light. Not the light of the sun, but rather that light which—through which in which—every soul had, and has and ever had, its being. 5246-1

PAGE 15:

God said, "Let there be life" and there WAS life! 364-7

Let it be remembered, or not confused, that the EARTH was peopled by ANIMALS before peopled by man! 364-6

PAGE 17:

There are the purposes for each entity's experience in materialization, or in that man calls life. For, life itself is the manifestation of God among man, in whatever form it may take. For life, life force, is an expression of love. Hence each soul is given the opportunity for the manifestation that it may be one with that Creative Force; knowing itself - in Him - to BE itself, and yet one with that Creative Force or God. 2402-2

….the purpose of the spirit entering into what we know as matter is a different condition or phase of condition from the purpose of entering into spirit as He is Spirit.

As those influences or forces entered that took man away FROM Him, then it was from that consciousness or spirit that the individuality had its source, its essence, its influence that might be made a personality in its activity. 262-119

For, ALL that ever was and ever is to be learned is that "The Lord thy God is one - ONE." O that it could and would be manifested … to bring to the consciousness of those it meets, that law "The Lord thy God is one." No matter in what clime, under what name, all must come to that as was from the beginning. 2402-2

PAGES 18 & 19:

Then came materiality as such into the earth, through the Spirit pushing itself into matter. 5246-1

These took on MANY sizes as to stature, from that as may be called the midget to the giants - for there were giants in the earth in those days, men as tall as (what would be termed today) ten to twelve feet in stature, and in proportion - well proportioned throughout. 364-11

…there were those who were physically entangled in the animal kingdom with the appendages, with cloven hoofs, with four legs, with portions of trees, with tails, with scales…that Thought Forms had so indulged in as to separate the purpose of God's creation of man as man—not as animal. 2072-8

Q) Were the thought forms that were able to push themselves out of themselves inhabited by souls, or were they of the animal kingdom? (A) That as created by that CREATED, of the animal kingdom. That created as by the Creator, with the soul. 364-7

PAGE 20:

The Soul could not express very well in the earth without a Covering; so it gradually took onto itself a Physical Body. Hence in the present Body our Soul shines through or is expressed through our outer Covering. 281-63

Individuals in the beginning were more of thought forms than individual entities with personalities as seen in the present. 364-10

PAGE 21:

Q) Were the thought forms that were able to push themselves out of themselves inhabited by souls, or were they of the animal kingdom? (A) That as created by that CREATED, of the animal kingdom. That created as by the Creator, with the soul. 364-7

The purpose of the entity in the earth is that is may know itself, also to be itself..fulfilling those purposes for which the entity comes into the earth, accepting, believing, knowing then thy relationship to that Creative Force. 3508-6

PAGE 22:

In the period, then - some hundred, some ninety-eight thousand years before the entry of Ram into India [See 364-3, Par. R2] - there lived in this land of Atlantis one Amilius [?], who had first NOTED that of the separations of the beings as inhabited that portion of the earth's sphere or plane of those peoples into male and female as separate entities, or individuals. As to their forms in the physical sense, these were much RATHER of the nature of THOUGHT FORMS, or able to push out OF THEMSELVES in that direction in which its development took shape in thought. 364-3

PAGE 23:

Amilius [?] - Adam, as given - first discerned that from himself, not of the beasts about him, could be drawn - WAS drawn - that which made for the propagation OF beings IN the flesh, that made for that companionship as seen by creation in the material worlds about same. 364-5

(Q) How long did it take for the division into male and female? (A) That depends upon which, or what branch or LINE is considered. When there was brought into being that as of the projection of that created BY that created, this took a period of evolutionary - or, as would be in the present year, fourscore and six year. That as brought into being as was of the creating OF that that became a portion of, OF that that was already created by the CREATOR, THAT brought into being as WERE those of the forces of nature itself. God said, "Let there be light" and there WAS light! God said, "Let there be life" and there WAS life! 364-7

(Q) Explain the "Sons of God - Daughters of Men - Sons of Man." (A) …. the influences of those souls that sought material expression pushed themselves into thought forms in the earth…. Then, as those expressed they were called the Sons of the Earth or Sons of Man. When the Creative Forces, God, made then the first man - or God-man - he was the beginning of the Sons of God. 262-119

Q) How is the legend of Lilith connected with the period of Amilius? (A) In the beginning, as was outlined, there was presented that that became as the Sons of God, in that male and female were as one, with those abilities for those changes as were able or capable of being brought about. In the changes that came from those THINGS, as were of the projections of the abilities of those entities to project, this as a being came as the companion; and when there was that turning to the within, through the sources of creation, as to make for the helpmeet of that as created by the first cause, or of the Creative Forces that brought into being that as was made, THEN - from out of self - was brought that as was to be the helpmeet, NOT just companion of the body. Hence the legend of the associations of the body during that period before there was brought into being the last of the creations, which was not of that that was NOT made, but the first of that that WAS made, and a helpmeet to the body, that there might be no change in the relationship of the SONS of God WITH those relationships of the sons and daughters of men. 364-7

PAGES 24 & 25:

Then there came that as sought for self-indulgence, self-glorification, and there was the beginning of warring among themselves for activity—still in Spirit. 262-114

The Sons of Belial were of one group, or those that sought more the gratifying, the satisfying, the use of material things for self, WITHOUT thought or consideration as to the sources of such nor the hardships in the experiences of others. Or, in other words, as we would term it today, they were those without a standard of morality. 9. The other group - those who followed the Law of One - had a standard. The Sons of Belial had no standard, save of self, self-aggrandizement. 877-26

Their STANDARD was that the soul was given by the Creator or entered from outside sources INTO the projection of the MENTAL and spiritual self at the given periods. THAT was the standard of the Law of One, but was REJECTED by the Sons of Belial. 877-26

PAGE 27:

Of the dust of the earth was the body-physical created. But the WORD, the MIND, is the controlling factor of its shape, its activity, from the source, the spiritual—the spiritual entity. 263-13

PAGE 28:

When the earth brought forth the seed in her season, and man came in the earth plane as the lord of that in that sphere, man appeared in five places then at once - the five senses, the five reasons, the five spheres, the five developments, the five nations. 5748-1

Before that we find that the entity was in the Beginning, when the sons of God came together to announce to Matter a way being opened for the souls of men, the souls of God's creation, to come again to the awareness of their error. 2156-2

(Q) Are the following the correct places? Atlantean, the red. (A) Atlantean and American, the red race. Q) Upper Africa for the black? (A) Or what would be known now as the more WESTERN portion of upper Egypt for the black. You see, with the changes - when there came the uprisings in the Atlantean land, and the sojourning southward - with the turning of the axis, the white and yellow races came more into that portion of Egypt, India, Persia and Arabia. 364-13

Page 29:

…man entered as man, through the MIND of the maker, see? In the form of flesh MAN, that which carnally might die, decay, become dust, entering into material conditions. The Spirit the gift of God, that man might be the One with Him, with the concept of man's creative forces throughout the physical world. Man, in Adam (as a group; not as an individual), entered into the world (for he entered in five places at once, we see - called Adam in one, see?) 900-227

   The ones that became the most USEFUL were those as would be classified (or called in the present) as the IDEAL stature, that was of both the male and female (as those separations had been begun); and the most ideal (as would be called) was Adam, who was in that period when he (Adam) appeared as five in one—See? 364-11

Page 30:

   When there was in the beginning a man's advent into the plane known as earth, and it became a living soul, amenable to the laws that govern the plane itself as presented, the Son of man entered earth as the first man. Hence the Son of man, the Son of God, the Son of the first Cause, making manifest in a material body. This was not the first spiritual influence, spiritual body, spiritual manifestation in the earth, but the first man - flesh and blood; the first carnal house, the first amenable body to the laws of the plane in its position in the universe. FOR, THE EARTH IS ONLY AN ATOM IN THE UNIVERSE OF WORLDS! 5749-3

   (Q) Describe the earth's surface at the period of the appearance of the five projections. (A) This has been given. In the first, or that known as the beginning, or in the Caucasian and Carpathian, or the Garden of Eden, in that land which lies now much in the desert, yet much in mountain and much in the rolling lands there. The extreme northern portions were then the southern portions, or the polar regions were then turned to where they occupied more of the tropical and semi-tropical regions;

hence it would be hard to discern or disseminate the change. The Nile entered into the Atlantic Ocean. What is now the Sahara was an inhabited land and very fertile. What is now the central portion of this country, or the Mississippi basin, was then all in the ocean.... The oceans were then turned about; they no longer bear their names, yet from whence obtained they their names? 364-13

PAGE 31:

He, that Christ-Consciousness, is that first spoken of in the beginning when God said, "Let there be light, and there was light." And that is the light manifested in the Christ. First it became physically conscious in Adam. And as in Adam we all die, so in the last Adam - Jesus, becoming the Christ - we are all made alive. Not unto that as of one, then. For we each meet our own selves, even as He; though this did not become possible, practical in a world experience, until He, Jesus, became the Christ and made the way. 2879-1

PAGE 32:

Hence the legend of the associations of the body during that period before there was brought into being the last of the creations, which was not of that that was NOT made, but the first of that that WAS made, and a helpmeet to the body, that there might be no change in the relationship of the SONS of God WITH those relationships of the sons and daughters of men. 364-7

ZECHARIA SITCHIN QUOTATIONS FROM
THERE WERE GIANTS UPON THE EARTH

PAGE 30:

The coronation of Marduk is taking place on Nibiru, and it is followed by an assembly of the gods assigned to Earth…. In the Below - on Earth - Marduk says, he has created Firm Ground suitable for a new Home….As the gathered gods rejoice at hearing Marduk'e project to establish Babylon, he went on to assign them their duties…. Six hundred, the Anunnaki 'of Heaven *and* Earth,' will be stationed on Earth itself. *pp. 125-126*

The *Atra-Hasis Epic i*n fact tells the story of a mutiny of the Anunnaki who refused to go on working in the gold mines and the ensuing chain of unintended consequences. p. 146

Anu summoned the Council of State. They found that the Anunnaki's complaints were justified; but how could the vital gold-supply mission be abandoned?….We have with us Ninmah; she is *Belet-ili,* a Birth-Giving goddess—

Let her fashion a *Lulu*,

Let an *Amelu* bear the toil of the gods1

Let her create a *Lulu Amelu*,

Let him bear the yoke!

He was suggesting to create a *Lulu*—a "Mixed One," a hybrid—to be an *Amelu,* a workman to take over the Anunnaki's toil. p. 147

The creation of *Adamu* took place 300,000 years ago (445,000—144,000)—exactly when *Homo Erectus* suddenly changed to *Homo sapiens*….. By mixing genes extracted from the blood of a god with the 'essence' of an existing earthly being, 'The Adam" was genetically engineered. There was no 'Missing Link" in our jump from Homo Erectus to Homo sapiens, because the Anunnaki jumped the gun on Evolution through genetic engineering. p. 149

www.ingramcontent.com/pod-product-compliance
Lightning Source LLC
Chambersburg PA
CBHW050805220426
43209CB00088BA/1639